MW01434922

8th House Publishing
Montreal, Canada

Copyright © 8th House Publishing 2014

First Edition

All rights reserved under International and Pan-American Copyright Conventions. No part of this book may be reproduced in any form or any electronic or mechanical means, including information storage and retrieval systems, without permission in writing from the publisher, except by a reviewer, who may quote brief passages in a review.

Published in Canada by 8th House Publishing.
Front Cover Artwork by 8th House Publishing

Designed by 8th House Publishing.
www.8thHousePublishing.com

Set in Raleway, BorisBlackBoxx and Delinquente.

Library and Archives Canada Cataloguing in Publication

Siqueiros, Damian, 1980-
[Photographs. Selections]
    To Russia with love / Damian Siqueiros.

ISBN 978-1-926716-33-6 (pbk.)

    1. Siqueiros, Damian, 1980-. 2. Gays--Russia (Federation)--Portraits. 3. Photography, Artistic. I. Title.

TR647.S586 2015   779.092   C2015-901900-1

To Russia with Love

DAMIAN SIQUEIROS

DAMIAN SIQUEIROS:
TO RUSSIA WITH LOVE

For artist-photographer Damian Siqueiros, feeling juxtaposed between two worlds is commonplace. Raised in Baja California, a great nephew of Mexican muralist David Alfaro Siqueiros, Damian began a serious study of fine art, in Paris, at an early age. As he became fully trilingual (in English, Spanish and French), the young Siqueiros began a concurrent fascination with the painterly possibilities of photography.

With a French-inflected passion for lenses and lighting, Siqueiros opened a studio in Montreal, where he has been shooting commercial work as resident photographer for the Montreal Ballet, as well as personal fine art projects.

Siqueiros' productions – and that is what they are, productions – are rich in artistic references and homages to classical painters and paintings. He casts his often gender-ambiguous models as actors who he then directs to emotionalize and physicalize the highly theatrical presence he captures on camera. Siqueiros builds sets, uses stylists, employs costumers and make-up artists, to anoint with great elegance and visual virtuosity those he has chosen to photograph. Then the artist caresses his subjects with a highly theatrical point of view to affect his vision. And, oh! What a vision Siqueiros has!

This artist begins working in *pre-production* on concept themes and sketches; in *production*, like a filmmaker he uses his cast and crew to lay down *the shot*; and finally, in *post-production*, Siqueiros uses computer techniques to merge backgrounds and architectural fantasies into his images, bringing them to their full presentational state. Siqueiros' photographs are extravagant mirages often featuring Jungian and Freudian subtexts.

Damian Siqueiros is an artist whose images work on many levels simultaneously. No mere collector of visual object trouvé documents, Siqueiros' pictures are exquisitely detailed, carefully planned out historical and artistic allegories. Siqueiros' works call to life iconic archetypes, myths and fantasies, costumed, bathed in light, color and glamour, so they all sing the artist's manifesto: *La beauté sauvera le monde!* Beauty will save the world!

—Phil Tarley, *Artists Corner Gallery Hollywood California*

To Russia With Love:
REPRESENTING RUSSIA'S QUEER HISTORY.

Damian Siqueiros, a Montreal-based visual artist and self-proclaimed "photopainter", imagines, captures and restores the queer of Russia with his project *To Russia With Love*. A field of inquiry tabooed for so long, the queer of Russia has not enjoyed a proper chance to be discussed or shown. To Russia With Love is a series of provocative compositions imbued with iconic symbolism. It is a meditative journey into the worlds of past and present, the worlds of censorship and merciless repression, which nonetheless produced some of the world's most dazzling artistic innovators.

The line-up of the characters who inhabit Siqueiros' imaginary and yet historically significant world is impressive: Piotr Ilich Tchaikovsky and his beloved companion Aleksey Sofronov; Sergei Diaghilev (the founder of Ballets Russes in Paris and arguably the first modern impresario at large) accompanied by his lover and muse Vaslav Nijinsky, a dancer and a choreographer, whose sheer audacity and force continue to live on as formative stimuli for the modern dance stage; and ultimately, two men behind the masks of Joseph Stalin and Vladimir Putin, the stars in their own right, the champions of censorship, repression, and homophobic rage.

Siqueiros explains his inspiration: "If we think in modern terms, Tchaikovsky is probably one of the most successful gay musicians who ever lived. His *Nutcracker* and *The Swan Lake* are embedded in our popular culture more than a century after his death. His life is intriguing, mysterious (his death claimed to be either a suicide or a murder) and his sexuality a topic of fascination. One of the things that is so crucial for me, is the effort by the Russian authorities to erase his queerness as if it was a stain on a nation itself. It is an attempt as futile as trying to cover the sun with one finger."

Indeed, the official Russian state today continues to deny and obliterate its past and present queer heroes. Notably, a recent documentary about Tchaikovsky produced in Russia – with generous state funding – achieves just that: denial and obliteration. Consider statements by the film's screenwriter, Yuri Arabov: *"It is far from a fact that Tchaikovsky was a homosexual. Only philistines think this. What philistines believe should not be shown in films."*

Now consider this letter Tchaikovsky penned to his brother Modeste, who, as we know now, was not so straight himself: *"I am now going through a very critical period of my life. I will go into more detail later, but for now I will simply tell you, I have decided to get married. It is unavoidable. I must do it, not just for myself but for you, Modeste, and all those I love. I think that for both of us our dispositions are the greatest and most insuperable obstacle to happiness, and we must fight our natures to the best of our ability. So far as I am concerned, I will do my utmost to get married this year, and if I lack the necessary courage, I will at any rate abandon my habits forever. Surely you realize how painful it is for me to know that people pity and forgive me when in truth I am not guilty of anything. How appalling to think that those who love me are sometimes ashamed of me. In short, I seek marriage or some sort of public involvement with a woman so as to shut the mouths of assorted contemptible creatures whose opinions mean nothing to me, but who are in a position to cause distress to those near to me."*

The photographer also remarks: Diaghilev and Nijinsky called my attention because they are at the center of one of the most productive, creative artistic companies. Diaghilev creates this hub for talent of all sorts like it was not seen before with Picasso, Balanchine, Stravinsky, Chanel. Paris is an extremely tough city and here is this Russian producer at the head of the avant-garde of the art world. That is an extremely rare phenomenon. The Rite of Spring, with its polarizing success, it has become a rite of passage for choreographers till this day. In terms of Nijinsky, he's arguably the best male dancer of the first half of the twentieth century. He starts a tradition of male dancers followed by Nureyev and Baryshnikov. One has to wonder how much of their creative force was based on the strength of their love affair.

The historical continuity of To Russia With Love series is preserved through a thoughtful and carefully arranged symbolic setting: a backdrop of the Red Square; an Orthodox icon on the wall; an omnipresent trunk, fully packed and ready to follow its owners into exile. A tender touch between the men behind the masks of Joseph Stalin and Vladimir Putin projects both a revelation and a verdict within the context of these compelling symbols: the lifeless masks of cruelty and hate reiterate their only aspiration – possession of the Square so Red that one can hardly tell between the drops of rain or blood on its eternal stones.

Another couple in the series is Anna Yevreinova and Maria Feodorova, a powerful lesbian tandem of the fin de siècle Russia. Queer history, despite its queer title, remains heavily dominated by histories of white cisgender gay men, while the histories of lesbian women, queer persons of color and gender nonconforming individuals are often exiled to the margins of the mainstream discourse. Anna Yevreinova was an audacious editor and publisher, and one of the first Russian female lawyers, who lived openly with her female partner Maria Feodorova. By bringing them within his reconstruction, Siqueiros mends and heals this ongoing injustice, while bringing forward a queer history of love and courage.

Siqueiros' "photopainting" is a meticulous and complex methodology, which involves thorough research, both textual and visual, painstaking reconstruction, and ultimately the production of an original work of art that challenges its own references. "Photopainting" is a technique inspired by the postmodern practice of appropriation or post-production, and as such, it facilitates the reading of the work through iconographical interpretation. In Siqueiros' own words: "Allegory is a great tool to cite and to deconstruct. It allows me to represent what is not visible and to add an historical perspective to the images. This technique helps me to compare and understand different discourses within the many queer histories which exist."

Of special note is the artist's inspiration and masterful visual quotations from the tradition of the Russian Romanticism. Russian Romantics proposed the understanding of the world through the prism of emotion, be it love, joy, fear, or hate. Fear and hate continue to define the disastrous situation for the queer community in Russia today. Siqueiros' To Russia With Love reconstructs and reinforces desperately needed, yet viciously suppressed, values of love and freedom.

The artist's educated imagination lands him and us in Russia as it is a today, a police war mongering state that nonetheless enjoys impunity from the free speaking world. The bloody marriage of authority and patriotic mania is skillfully unraveled through intimate embrace between two women: a police officer and a Sochi Olympian– the true new Russian symbols, who nonetheless find themselves imprisoned by the never-ending past.

Denial and obliteration have always been a weapon of choice for stagnant inhumane autocracies. To Russia With Love exposes and educates, transmits and transforms, constructs and reconstructs key queer heroes of the Russian history through an astute and visually captivating mise en scène. If knowledge is power, than the acknowledgment of Russia's queer history may bring about a change in people's minds, their minds remaining a primary target where power always aims.

—**Ivan Savvine**, *Russian-American art historian, writer, and curator.*

To Russia with Love

DAMIAN SIQUEIROS

PHOTO SERIES

Tchaikovsky and his Lover (Akeksey Sofronov)　　　　　8

Anna Yevreinova and Maria Feodorova　　　　　12

Sergei Diaghilev and Vaslav Nijinsky　　　　　18

Policewoman and Olympic Athlete:　　　　　25

Joseph Stalin and Vladimir Putin　　　　　31

TABLE OF CONTENTS

Introduction	6
TO RUSSIA WITH LOVE	8
The Project	35
Defining a Style : Photo-painting & Russian Romanticism	36
Building the Images: The Process	37
The Situation	43
Project Mission	44
Reach-out Program	44
CREDITS	46
ABOUT THE AUTHOR	48

To Russia with Love / К России с любовью

Montreal artists supporting the Russian LGBT community.

THE PROJECT "TO RUSSIA WITH LOVE" was born of the realization that the real moral imperative is not to remain passive in the face of hatred and injustice. That's how a group of Montreal artists and collaborators united to stand against the recent wave of institutionalized homophobia and the ruthless violence that exists in Russia towards our gender diverse brothers and sisters.

"To Russia with Love" portrays iconic and historically relevant gay and lesbian Russians with their respective partners, starting from the 19th century to our time. The projects features Pyotr Tchaikovsky (composer) and his long time companion Akeksey Sofronov, Anna Yevreinova and Maria Feodorova (reputed lawyer and writer respectively from the 19 century), Sergei Diaghilev (founder of the Ballets Russes in Paris) and Vaslav Nijinsky, a contemporary fictional lesbian couple made of a police woman and an Olympic athlete and lastly a male couple impersonating Stalin and Putin.

These characters are without doubt some of Russia's precious children, but in their denial they downplay or erase their homosexual identities. The images of "To Russia with Love" not only validate those identities, but they bring them to the fore as the source of love, happiness and inspiration. Though the project highlights the intimacy of the couples' love, gay or straight, this love is not something to be kept within the walls of the bedroom, but to express in public and be enjoyed with freedom.

Damian Siqueiros

The couples are represented on a stage that resembles that of a photography studio at the end of the 19th century. The colors and elements of the image have been chosen carefully to reflect that era as well as the romantic hues of Russian art. We see unequivocally Russian elements, such as the contemporary flag or the St. Petersburg Cathedral and the religious icon. The latter stand as a symbol of the shameful role the church plays on the violence and collective homophobia of Russians.

The project is led by visual artist and photographer Damian Siqueiros, who has collaborated with prestigious magazines and clients such as *Vogue Mexico, Elle* and *Les Grands Ballets Canadiens*.

Siqueiros and his equally passionate collaborators believe that fighting hatred with hatred is as nonsensical as trying to extinguish a fire with gasoline. The project "To Russia with Love" does not seek to condemn those who perpetrate injustice, but to increase the value of love and to validate the couples and the identities of our Russian brothers and sisters from the LGBT community.

This is a particular time in history where Equality in rights for the LGBT community in which many modern societies have come to accept and cherish diversity, and on the other hand many others seem to participate in a backlash of enrooted homophobia and political diversions disguised as sanctified morality.

For more information : http://www.torussiawithloveproject.com

Contact : Damian Siqueiros t. 514 662 45 19 E-mail: damiansiqueiros.com

To Russia with Love / К России с любовью

Des artistes montréalais s'engagent pour les LGBT russes

LE PROJET «TO RUSSIA WITH LOVE» est né lorsqu'un groupe d'artistes et collaborateurs montréalais a compris qu'il ne fallait pas rester passif face à la récente vague d'homophobie institutionnalisée, cette violence impitoyable qui frappe, en Russie, les lesbiennes, gais, bisexuel(le)s et transsexuel(le)s (LGBT).

«To Russia with Love» montre, en photos, des gais et lesbiennes russes, du XIXe siècle à nos jours. Certains d'entre eux ont parfois marqué l'histoire de leur pays. Ainsi, on retrouve le compositeur Pyotr Tchaikovsky avec son compagnon Akeksey Sofronov, Anna Yevreinova and Maria Feodorova (une avocate réputée et une écrivaine du XIXe siècle), Sergei Diaghilev (fondateur des Ballets russes à Paris) et le danseur étoile Vaslav Nijinsky, un couple lesbien fictif composé d'une policière et d'une athlète olympique, enfin un couple gai personnifiant Staline et Vladimir Poutine.

Bien que le projet mette en lumière l'intimité de ces couples, l'amour, qu'il soit homosexuel ou hétérosexuel, n'est ici pas quelque chose qu'il faut à conserver entre les murs d'une chambre à coucher. Au contraire, il faut l'exprimer publiquement et en jouir librement.

Les couples sont représentés sur une scène qui ressemble à celle d'un studio de photos tel qu'on pouvait en trouver à la fin du XIXe siècle. Les couleurs et les éléments ont été choisis avec soin, pour refléter autant cette époque que les teintes romantiques de l'art russe. On peut clairement voir des éléments du patrimoine russe, comme le drapeau, la Cathédrale de Saint-Pétersbourg ou l'icone religieuse. Cette dernière symbolise le rôle honteux joué par l'Église dans la propagation de la violence et de l'homophobie collective des Russes.

Damian Siqueiros

L'artiste visuel et photographe Damian Siqueiros a dirigé ce projet. Par le passé, celui-ci a collaboré avec de prestigieux magazines et clients, comme Vogue Mexico, Elle et Les Grands ballets canadiens.

Pour Damian Siqueiros et ses collaborateurs, il est absurde de répliquer à la haine par la haine. Ce serait comme tenter d'éteindre un feu en déversant de l'essence. Voilà pourquoi «To Russia with Love» n'entend pas condamner ceux qui perpétuent l'injustice, mais plutôt privilégier des valeurs comme l'amour et mettre en lumière ces couples et les identités LGBT russes.

Dans les prochains mois, le projet «To Russia with Love» sera exposé aux États-Unis et au Québec. Grâce au soutien du magazine russe basé sur le territoire américain Depesha et à une campagne de levée de fonds sur Internet, une exposition sera organisée à New York, en juin 2014. Montréal accueillera celle-ci en mai 2015, à la Galerie Dentaire. Par ailleurs, une partie de l'argent récolté sera reversé à l'association «Russian LGBTQ Network» qui vient en aide aux minorités sexuelles en Russie. «To Russia with Love» bénéficie également du soutien de l'application gaie Hornet - 2,4 millions de contacts dans le monde, dont 200.000 à Moscou - qui fera la promotion du projet.

Pour plus d'information : http://www.torussiawithloveproject.com

Contact : Damian Siqueiros t. 514 662 45 19 E-mail: damiansiqueiros.com

Tchaikovsky & his lover (Akeksey Sofronov):

Tchaikovsky is without a doubt one of the most important composers of all times. His music, The Nutcracker and Swan Lake to name a few, are embedded in our minds and our culture. The composer was from the beginning a corner stone of the project. After more than a century of his death his sexuality is controversial still. By his own account, it is clear he was gay. It is well documented in his letter to his brother Modest who was also gay. Nonetheless, Russian authorities seem to ignore this and deny his sexual orientation. Russian society during Tchaikovsky's life was not as lenient as their counterparts in the rest of Europe. Homosexuality was a sin and crime punishable by exile and banishment from the Tsarist court, which in the case of the composer would mean the end of his career.

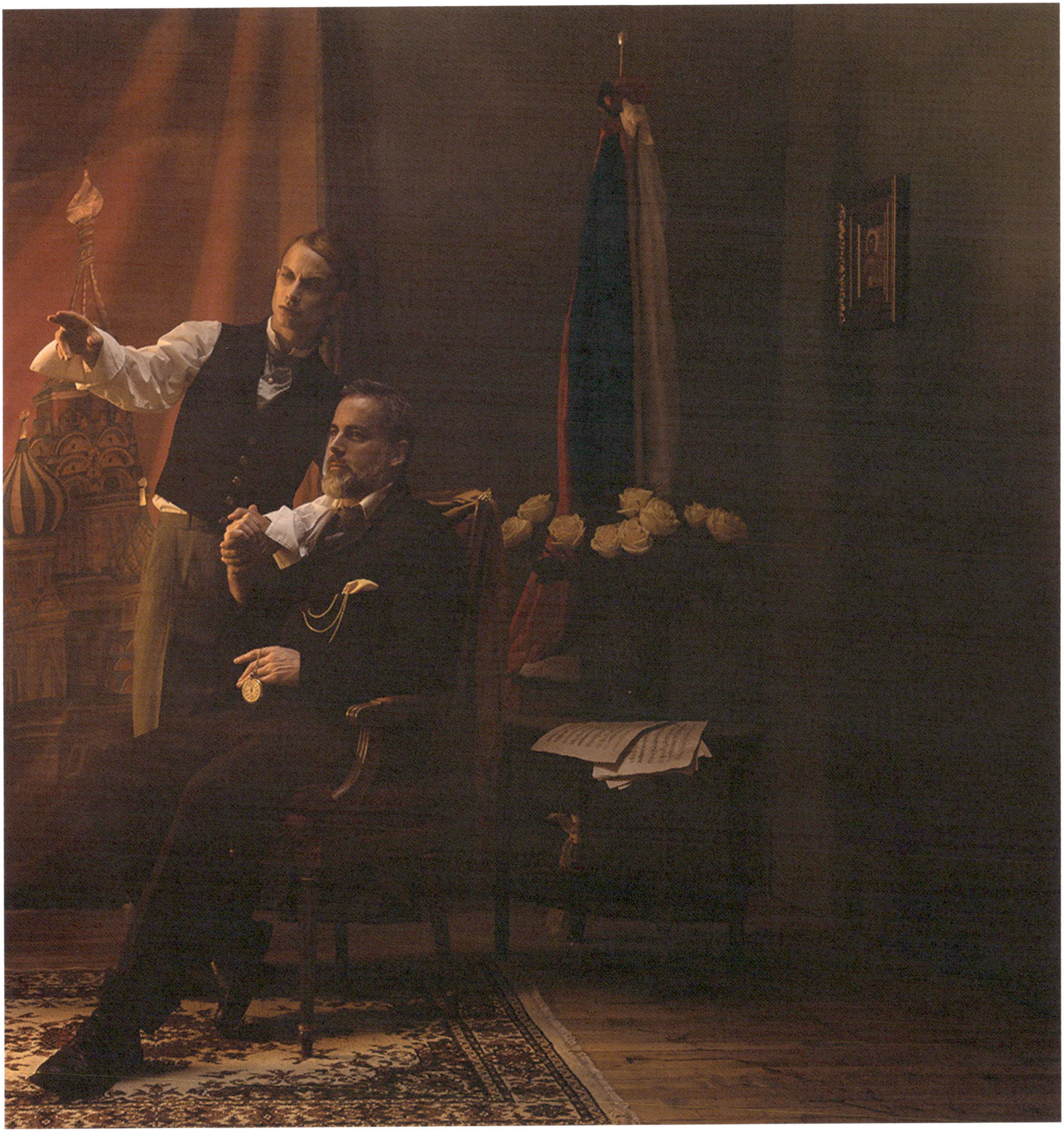

To Russia With Love

Tchaikovsky's attempts to lead a 'morally sound' life made his sexual orientation even more evident. He had many male lovers and his botched marriage lasted no more than a few months. At the end, he seemed to have made peace with his sexuality. His servant, lover and long time companion Akeksey Sofronov stayed with him until his death. Though he officially died from cholera, it has been suspected that he was bullied into suicide by drinking contaminated water. Tens of thousands of people attended his funeral; he was both a loved genius and a pariah.

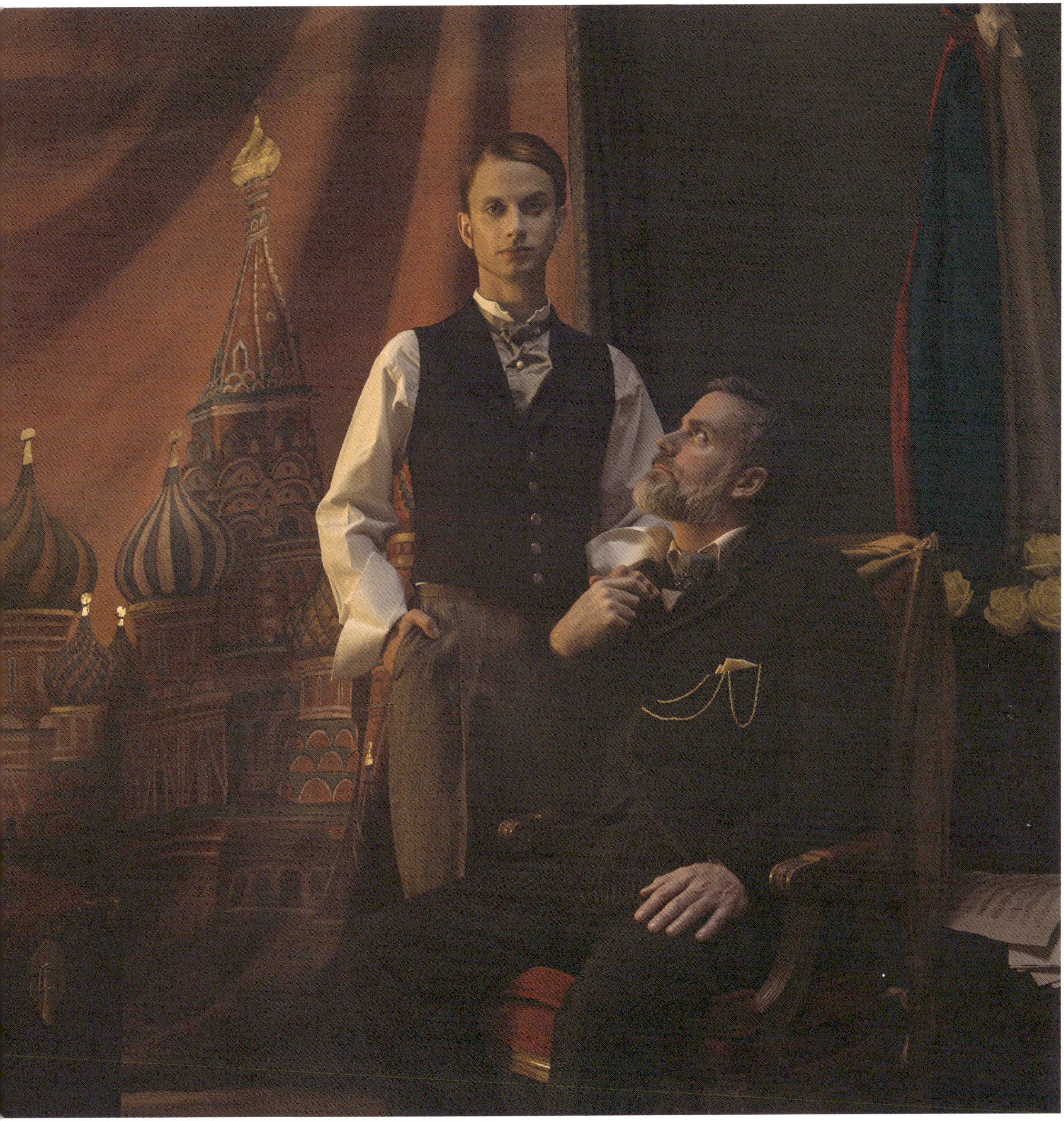

Anna Yevreinova & Maria Feodorova

Little information is available on this late 19-century lesbian couple. Nonetheless they seemed highly inspirational on several accounts. Anna Yevreinova was the first Russian woman to obtain a law degree (University of Leipzing). Along with her lover, author Maria Feodorova, they founded and ran the journal 'The Northern Herald'. They both fought for women's rights and lived together as a couple in an arrangement that defied the customs of the time.

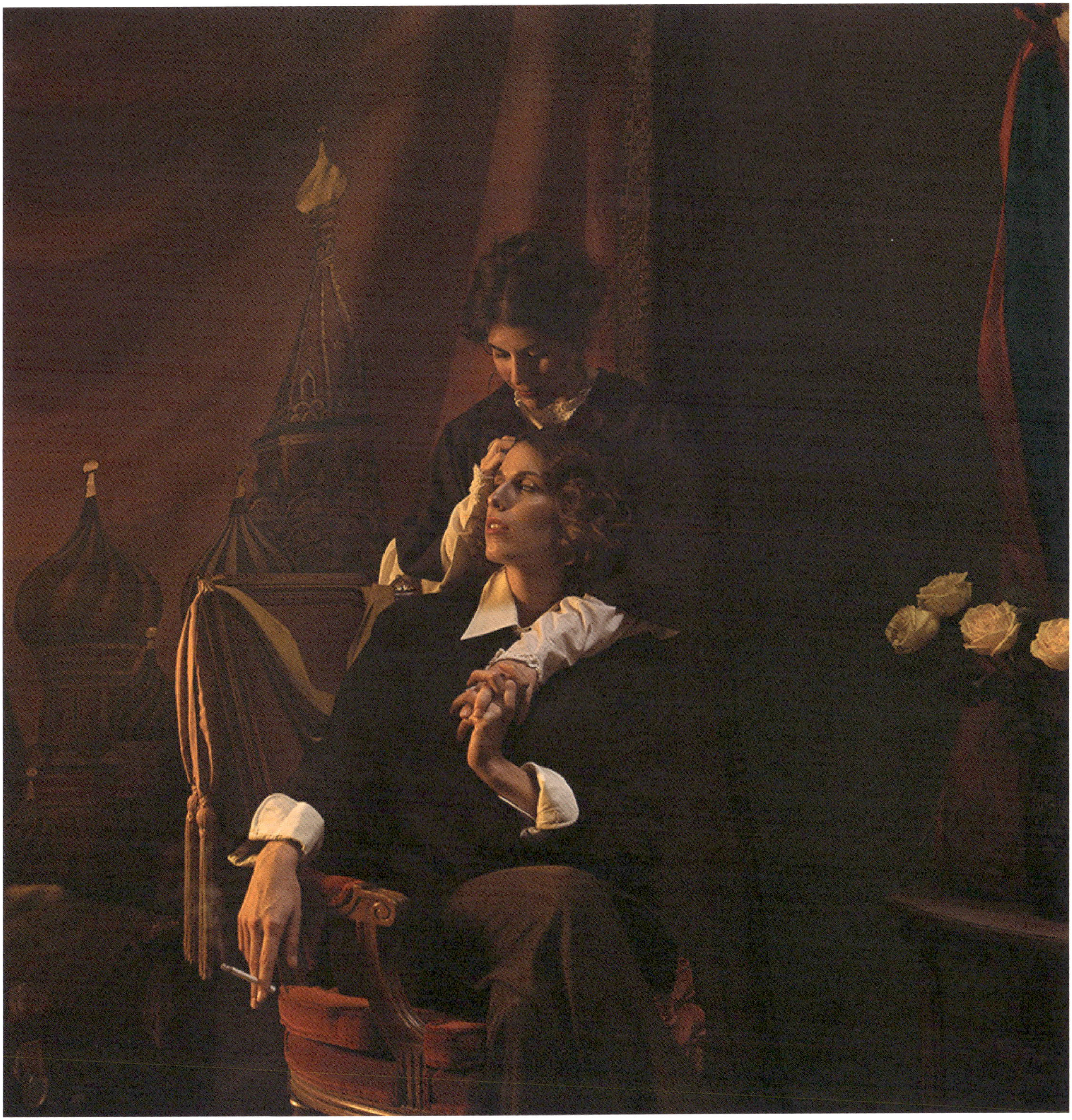

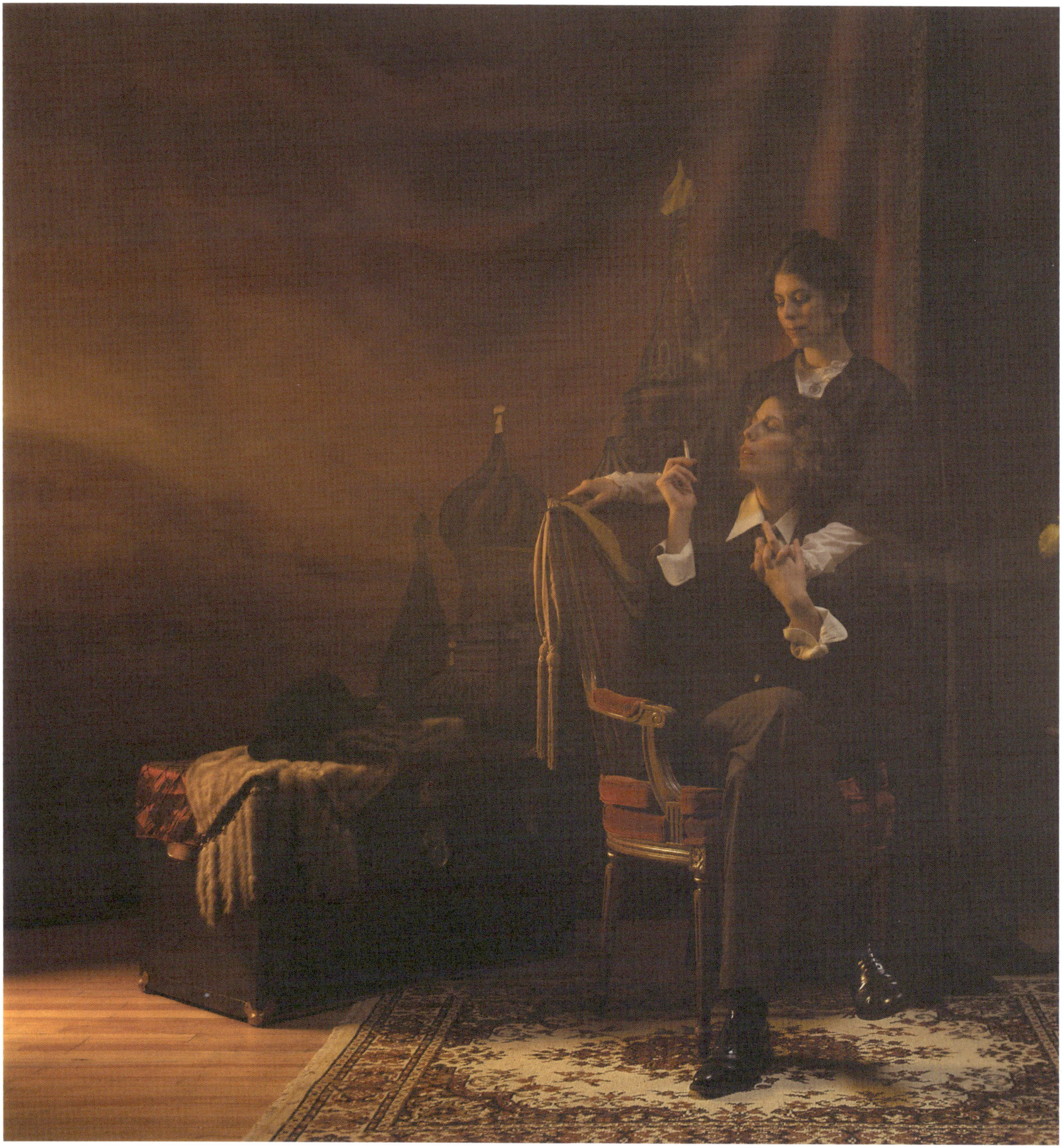

Damian Siqueiros

The image is inspired by real lesbian couples of the times, in which is was common to see one of the women wearing men's garb, in this case Feodorova. Yevreinova is dressed in a manner reminiscent of the suffragette movement in England at the beginning of the 20th century.

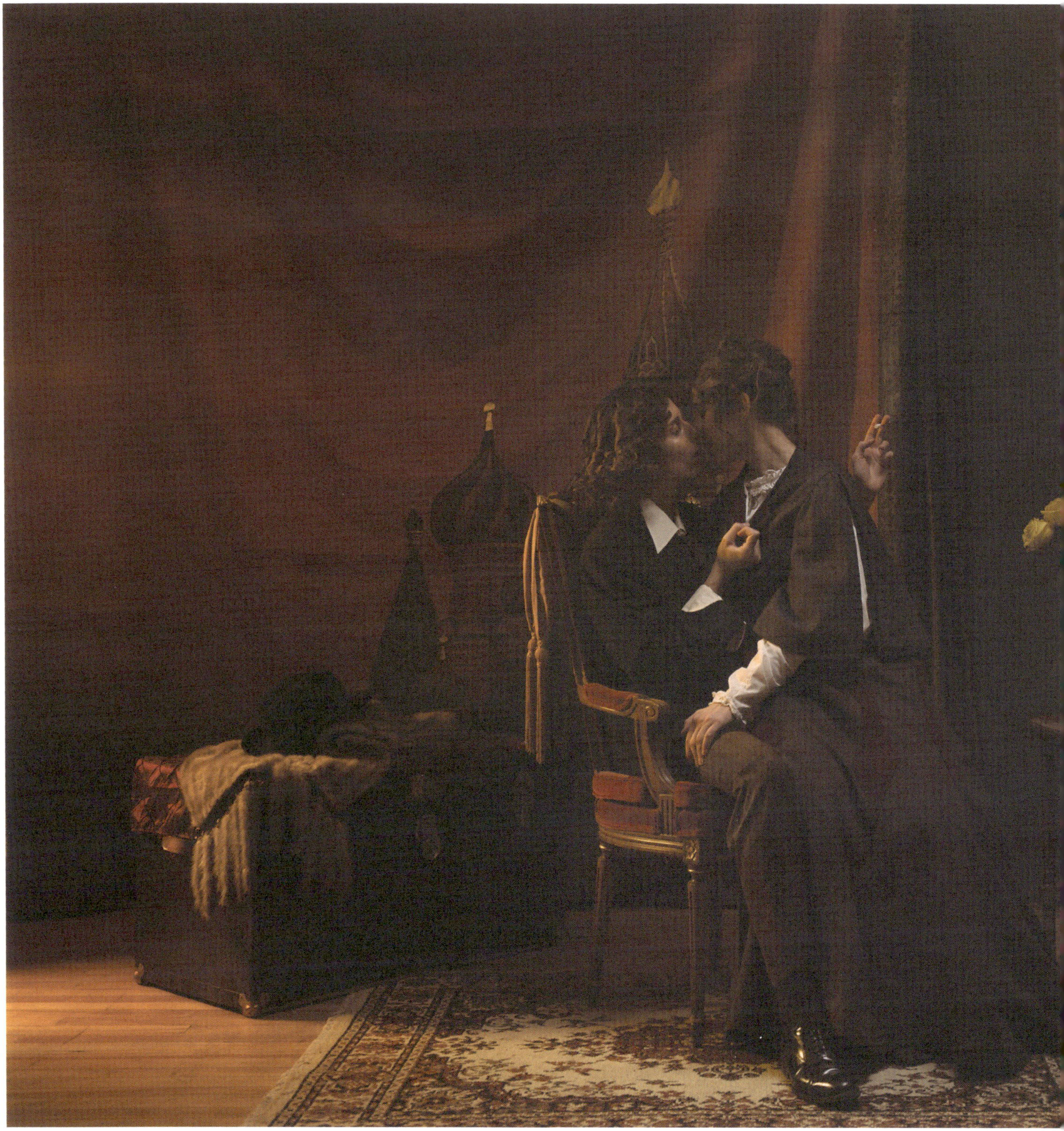

Damian Siqueiros

Through these images and the project in general, we intend to portray the intimacy of the couple, from a subtle touch to a kiss. We want to minimize the sexual innuendos without effacing them. Since many homophobic policies are based on the idea of traditional family values and reproduction and fertility, it was important to show that gay couples are like any other couple—they too can serve as the nucleus from which a family is formed.

Sergei Diaghilev & Vaslav Nijinsky

Les Ballets Russes dance company of Paris is unparalleled in its capacity to host so much of the outstanding talented artists that defined the 20th century. The company founded by the visionary Sergei Diaghilev in 1909, hosted artists like Picasso, Matisse, Stravinsky, Fokine and Coco Chanel.

Dancer Nijinsky reached a turning point in his life when he met Diaghilev. They became lovers and Nijinsky became the male star of *Les Ballets Russes*. With his exceptional talent and the help of his lover, Nijinksy became the most influential ballet dancer in the first half of the 20th century. The love affair came to an end when Nijinsky succumbed to social pressures and attempted to lead a traditional life and marry a woman. Though this created a major riff between the two men, Diaghilev never ceased to help Nijinsky in his life and career.

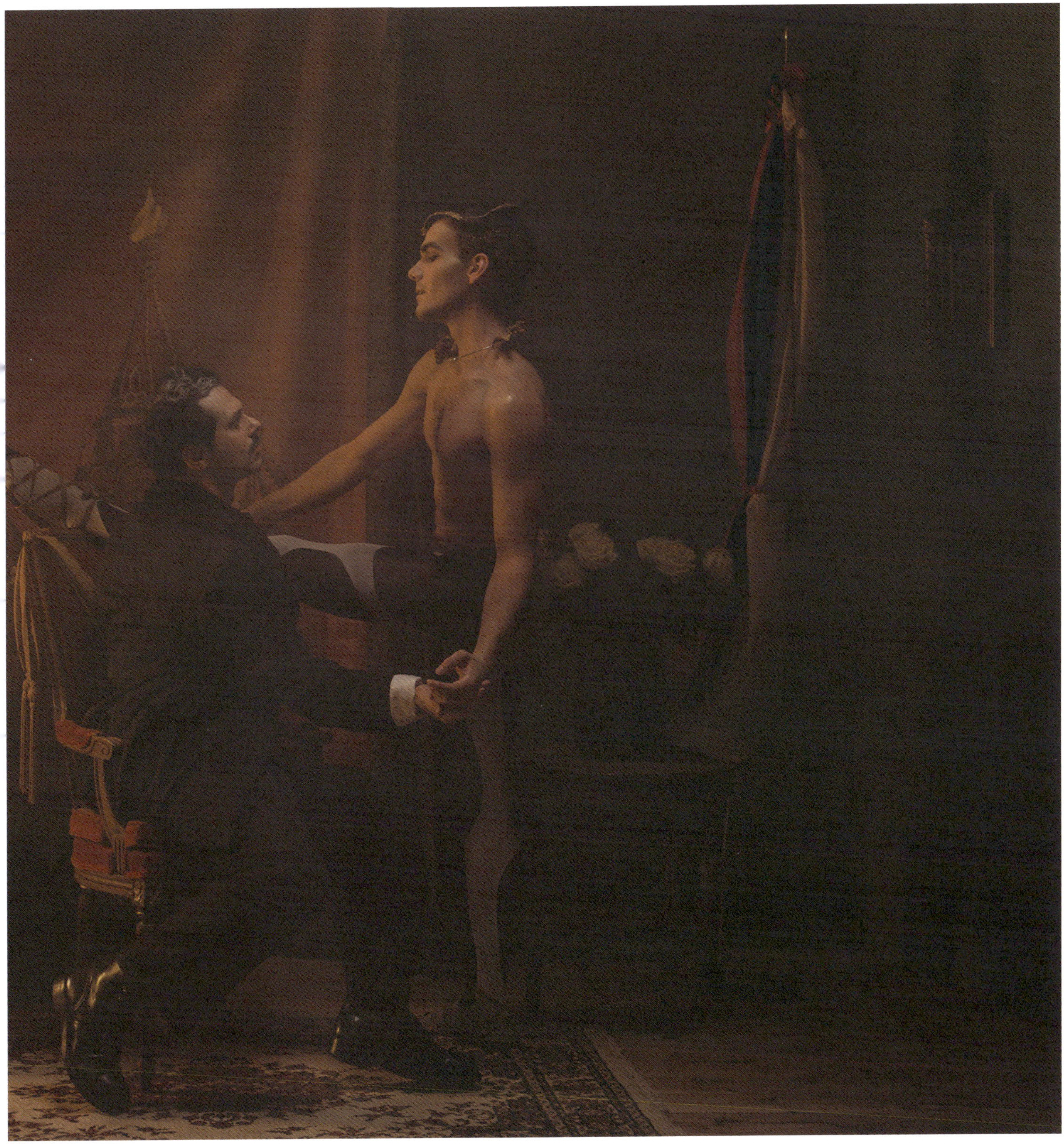

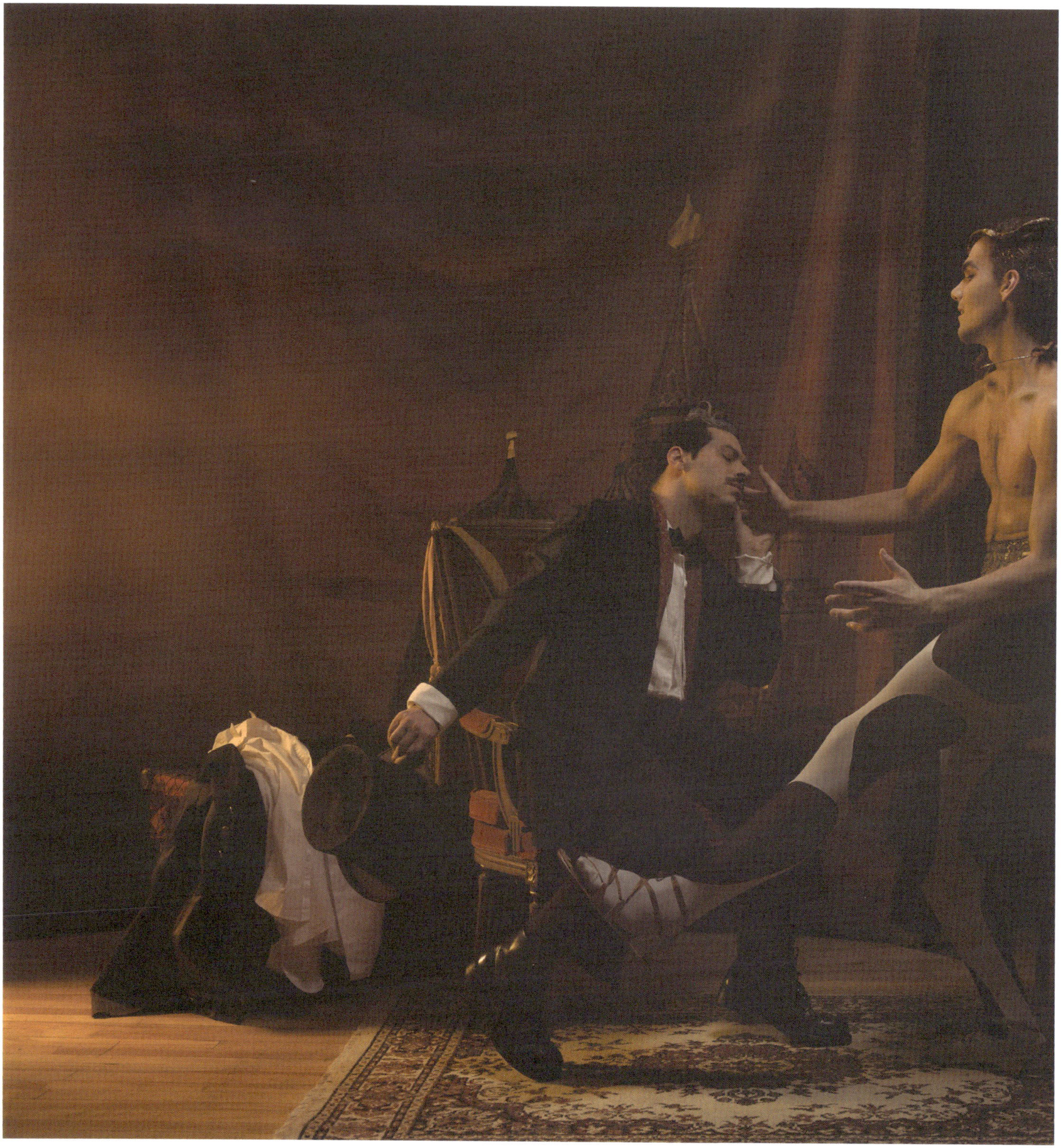

Damian Siqueiros

This scene depicted in "To Russia with Love" imagines them as they discuss one of Nijinsky's most famous roles in *L'après-midi d'un Faune*. In the background, on the chest, we see Nijinsky's day-to-day clothes as a reminder that this is a private performance for the man he loves.

To Russia With Love

The images represent the passionate, sexual, and loving nature of their relationship. It was important to highlight that both Diaghilev and Nijinsky were involved in the performing arts by showing the histrionic and erotic qualities of their personalities.

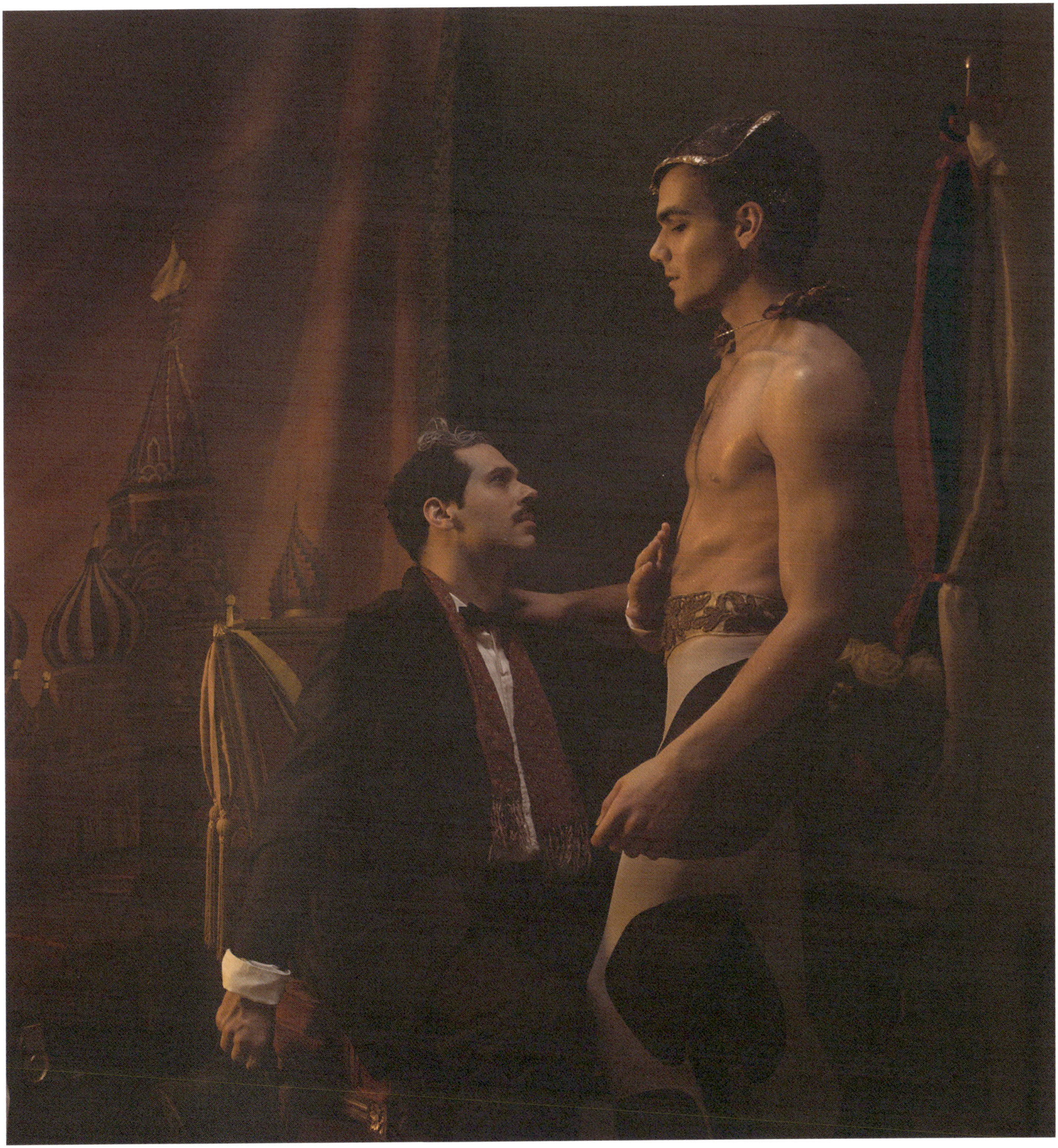

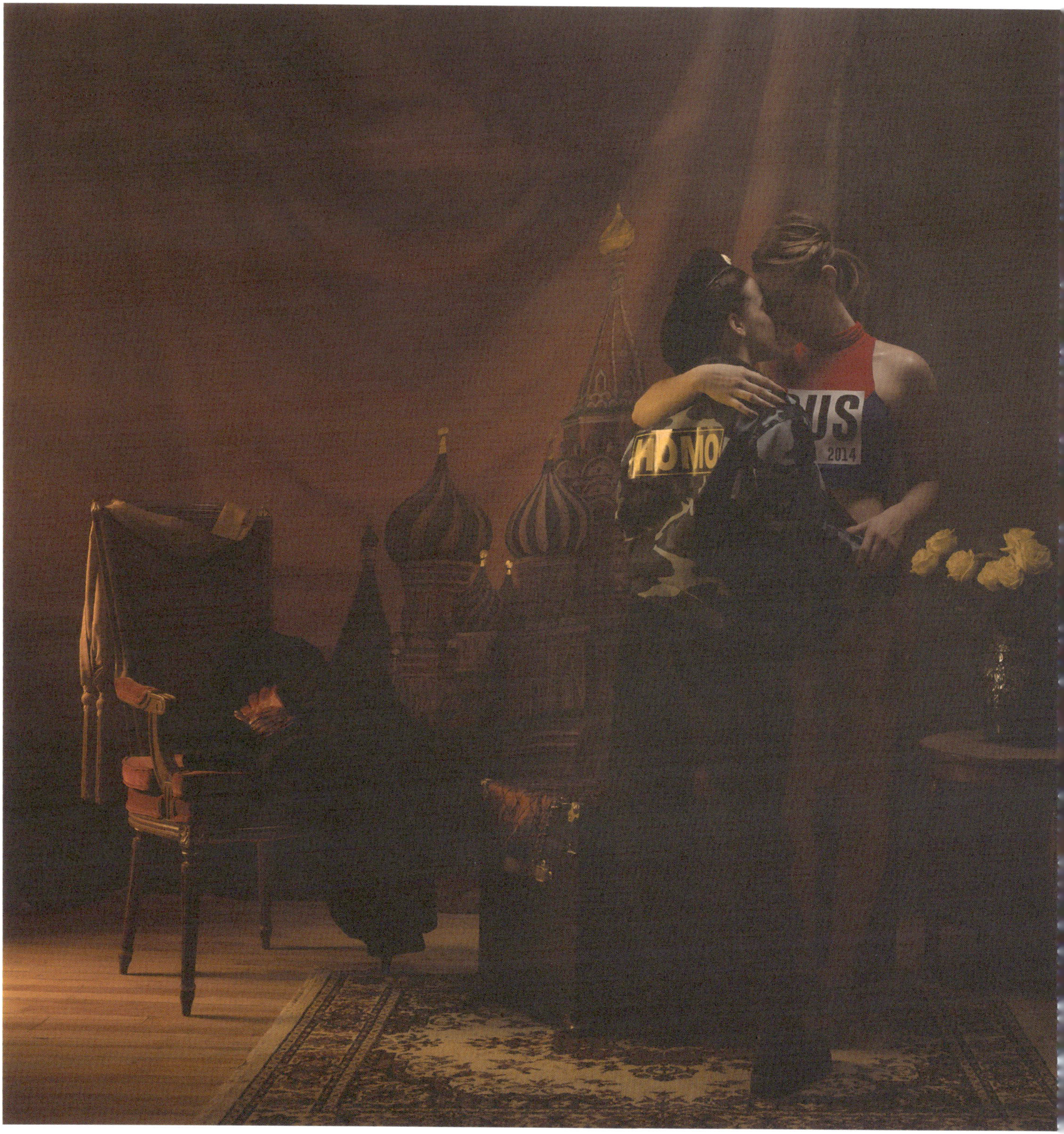
HOMO
US
2014

Damian Siqueiros

Policewoman & Olympic Athlete:

This tableau represents the rise of hope and defiance to the new draconian laws forbidding Russian non-traditional families of expressing their love and affection in public. The policewoman is a reminder of the historic and heavily militarized control Russia has over it's population. It also reminds us of the use of force in the repression of freedom of speech. The policewoman flirting with her partner is a symbol of a dwindling kind of power based on fear, violence and ultra-conservative values. She represents the possibility of change.

To Russia With Love

The figure of the athlete is symbolic as well, though it references real events. The most evident is a reminder of the past Olympic games putting Russia and their human rights issues at center stage. The athlete also echoes Tchaikovsky, in that they are both a symbol of pride and shame for their country.

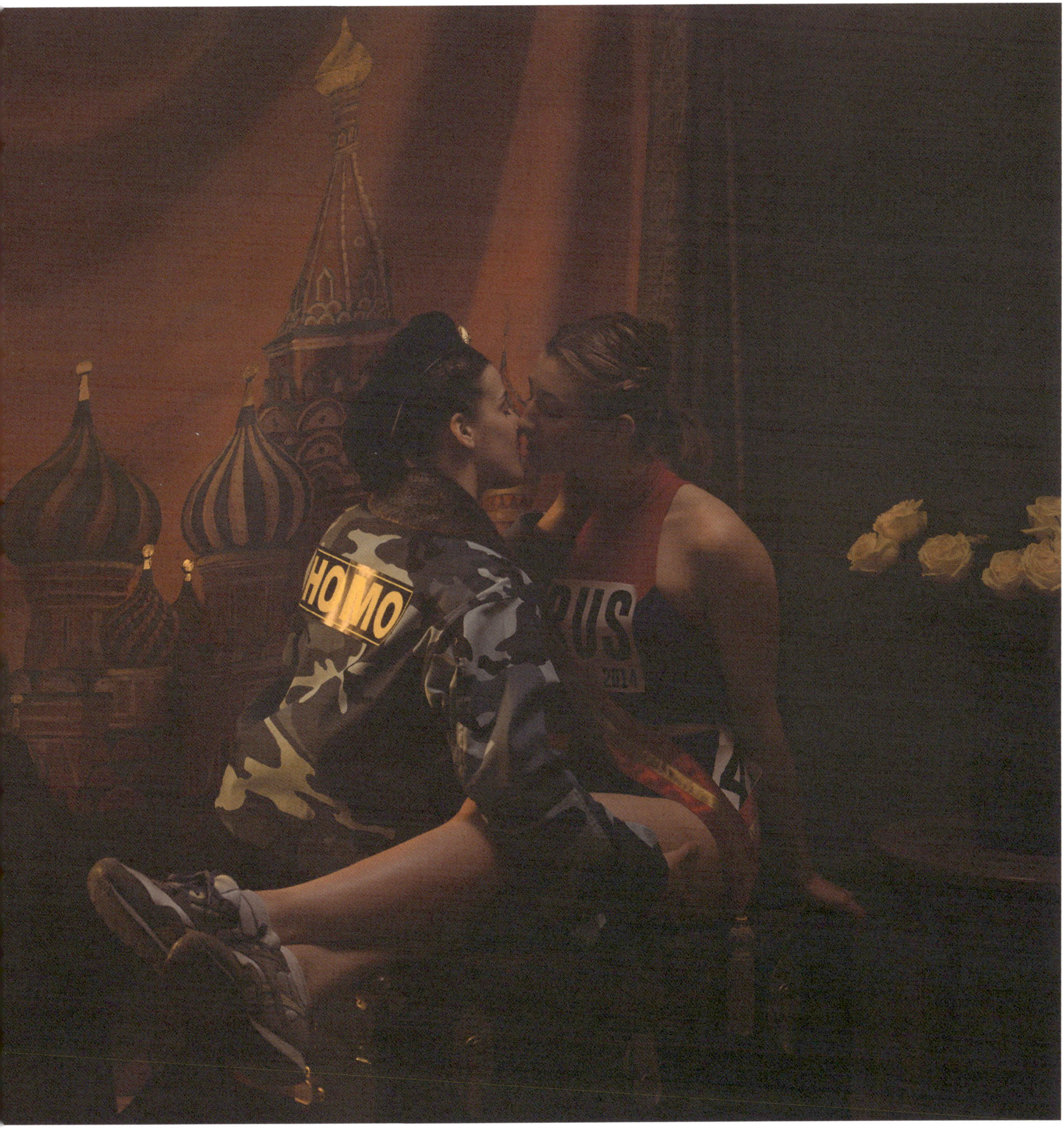
HOMO
RUS
2014

Irony is a powerful tool against oppressive regimes. We had noticed that the signs on the back of the jackets of the police force, when seen through the reflection of a mirror would say Homo, a common derogatory colloquialism or slang word to refer to homosexual people. We wanted to make it obvious by spelling it from left to right. It was a happy coincidence that the sign of the policewoman and that of the athlete put together read "Homo 'R' us". We are the homos; we are the dissenters; and we are taking control of our lives.

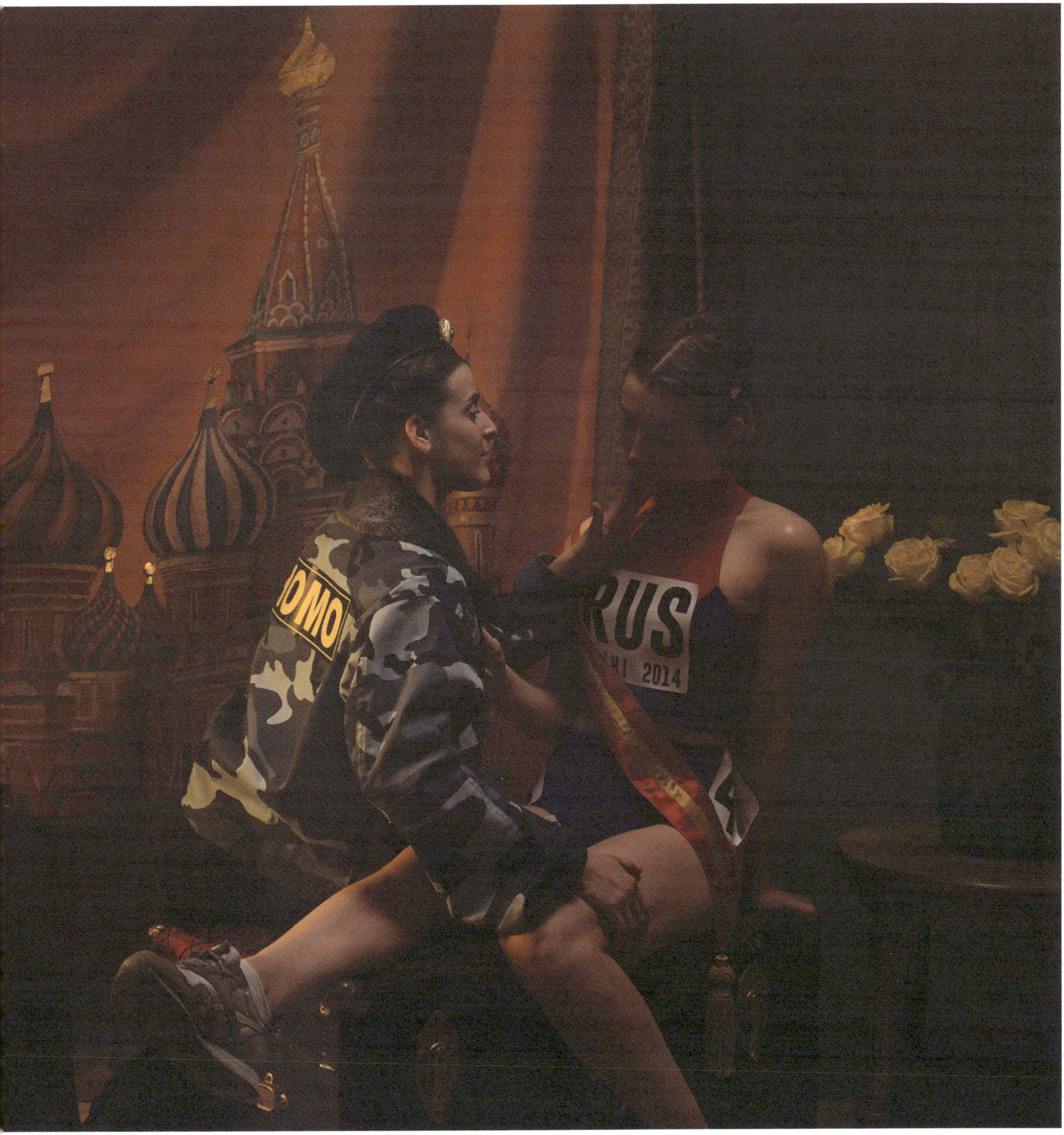
RUS
2014

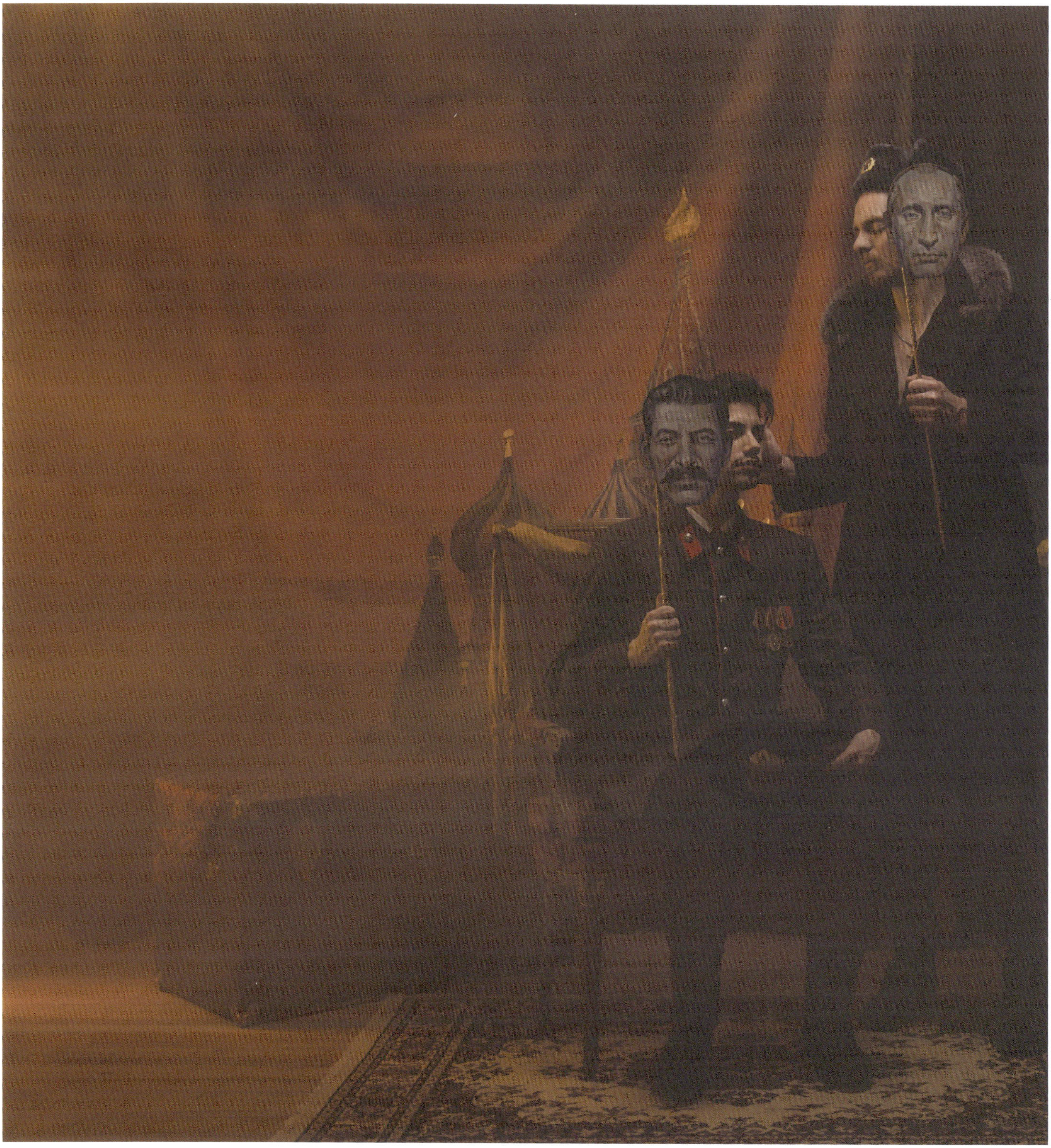

Damian Siqueiros

Joseph Stalin & Vladimir Putin

Just before Stalin came into power, the Communist Party under the leadership of Lenin, changed the tight laws of the Russian Civil code to accept less traditional family values and homosexuality was decriminalized in Russia. Unfortunately that didn't last long. Stalin and his dysfunctional rule reinstated the penalty for homosexual acts, mainly for political reasons. Male homosexuality was regarded as a sign of fascism and dissidence from the regime. Thousands of men were imprisoned under this law.

History seems to repeat itself with the current president Vladimir Putin. After the end of the Stalinist Era, a period of relative freedom and acceptance seemed to establish itself in Russia towards the 1970's. Then in the early 90's, under president Boris Yeltsin homosexuality was again decriminalized. Putin seems to have found in persecuting the LGBT community a powerful weapon to validate his power in the eyes of the public opinion, as 90% of Russians support the anti-gay propaganda law.

To Russia With Love

This tableau represents a paradox by portraying a loving gay couple in distress under the new laws, dressed in the guise of the two Russian rulers that have been the most abrasive towards the LGBT community.

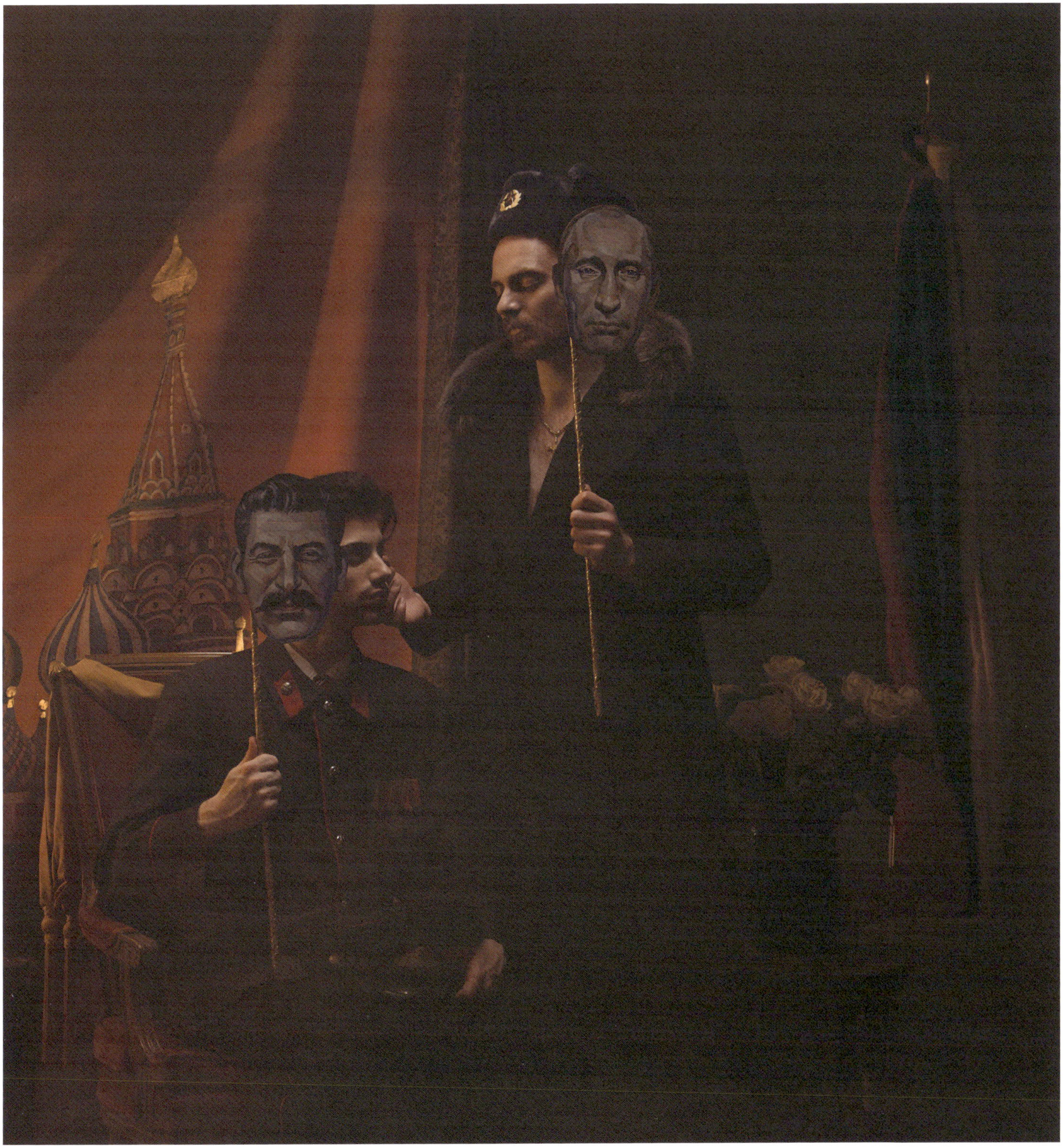

TO RUSSIA WITH LOVE
THE PROJECT

DEFINING A STYLE :
PHOTO-PAINTING & RUSSIAN ROMANTICISM

PHOTO-PAINTING (FORM and CONCEPT)
It is a technique inspired by the postmodern practice of appropriation or post-production.
• This technique facilitates the reading of the work through iconographical interpretation.
• The pictorial aesthetic seeks to soften the message.
• Allegory is a great tool to cite and to deconstruct. It allows the artist to represent what is not visible and to add an historical perspective to the images.
• This technique helps compare and understand different scopic regimes.

NATIONALIST ROMANTICISM
• Romanticism proposes the understanding of the world trough emotions, may these be positive or negative.
• Russian artist highlight historical topics and discover poetic themes ignored before. They are not confined to the representation of the visible.
• Realism and Naturalism where also influences for the project as they concentrate on the psychology of the characters.
• The 3 artistic movements are socially engaged with the historical, social an political ideas of their time.

Damian Siqueiros

BUILDING THE IMAGES: THE PROCESS

MAKE-UP

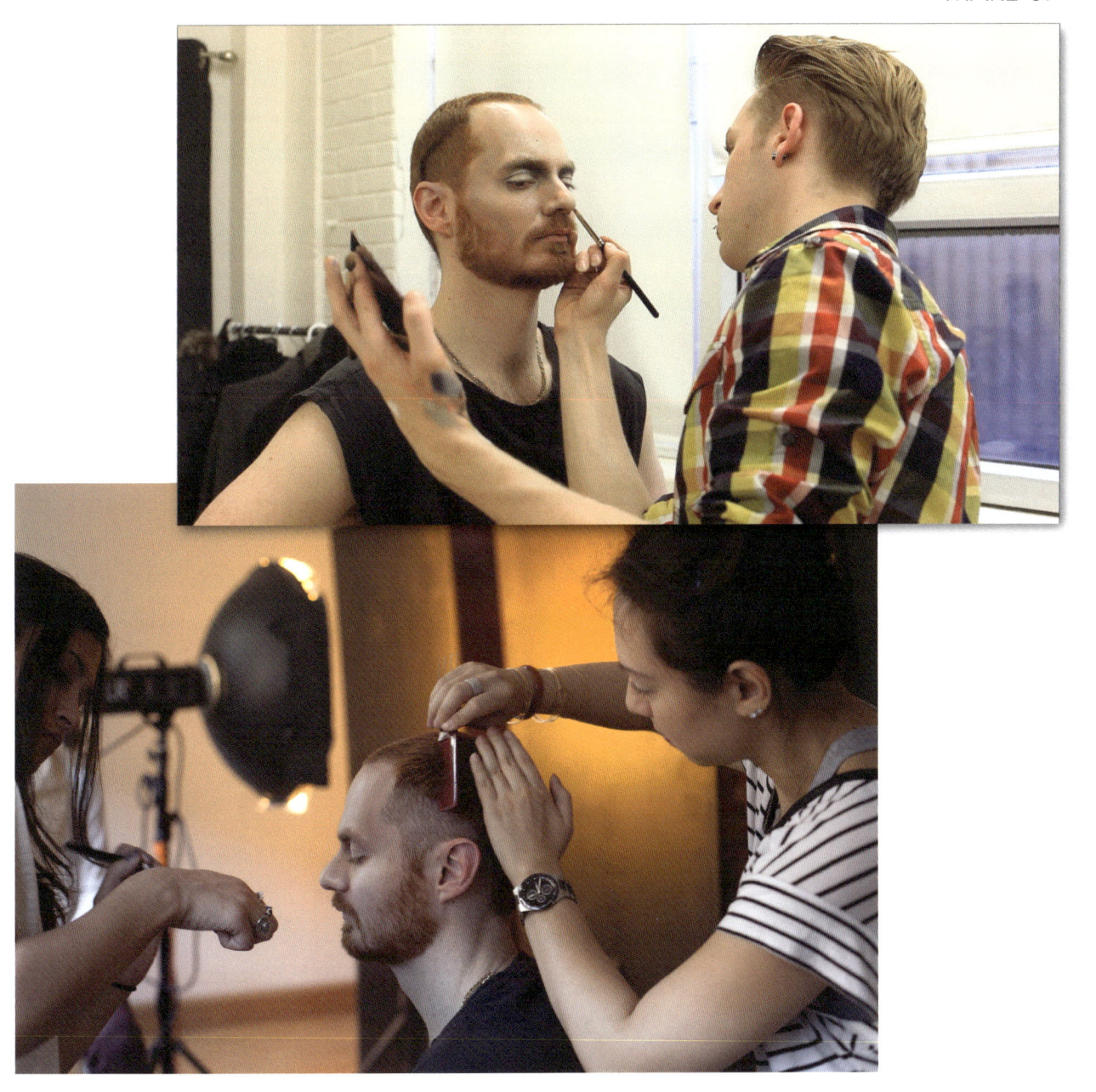

To Russia With Love

COSTUME

38

Damian Siqueiros

CREATING AN ATMOSPHERE

SET DESIGN

Damian Siqueiros

SCENE DESIGN

LIGHTING

THE TEAM

Credits from left to right: 1- Roscoe Stone (Nijinsky), 2 -Guillermo Castellanos (BTS video), 3- Diana Gonzalez Caballero (Assistant to production), 4- Miguel Doucet (Diaghilev), 5- Sophia Graziani (Stylist / Costume designer), 6-Olivier Vinet (Make-up Artist), 7- Damian Siqueiros (Photographer and Art Director), 8- Cathy L (Hair stylist), 9-Gigiola Caceres (2nd assistant), 10- Sebastien Beaupre (Stalin impersonator), 11- Camille Sabbagh (Assistant to styling and Make-up), 12- Bérenger Zyla (1st Assistant) Absent: Daniel Barkley (Painter- background and masks), Tristan Harris (Putin impersonator), Patricia Doss (Agent), Stephan Amnotte (Tchaikovsky), Rachel Salzman (Policewoman), Antonia Dolhaine (Athlete), Claire Crombez (Maria Feodorova), Evelyne-Louise Bergeron (Anna Yevreinova), Liliana Ortiz and Mateo H. Casis (BTS material), Antoine Aubert (Communications collaborator), Arnaud Baty (Graphic Design).

Damian Siqueiros

TO RUSSIA WITH LOVE
THE PROJECT

THE SITUATION

- Homosexuality was decriminalised in Russia in 1993 and taken-off the list of mental illnesses in 1999.
- The new anti-propaganda law doesn't use the word 'homosexual', it uses the euphemism 'non-traditional relationships'. 90% of Russians support the new law; 74% are against homosexuality and only 16% consider it acceptable.
- The new law is a cover up and a distraction for deeper social issues. The government promotes it as protection for children and traditional family values. A great deal of Russia's population associates homosexuality to pedophilia. We see proof of this in the warnings Putin makes to gay people: "Leave our children alone". Pinknews in the UK reports that President Putin claims that legalising paedophilia had seriously been considered in several countries in relation to their acceptance of gay rights.
- The new law incites extremist groups such as Occupy Pedophilia to take action into their hands.
- It is difficult to have an accurate idea of incidents of agression related to homophobia as they are usually not reported to the police. A poll by the LGBT Network afirms that 15.3% of LGBT people has suffered violence related to their gender. Often these attacks are reported under a pretence.
- Fines for people that challenge the laws can go from $150 to $28,000. 39.7% of LGBT people have had work-related issues because of their gender.
- Nobody dares show affection to a same sex partner in public, though this is not forbidden under the new law.
- A new law heading to the Russian Parliament would authorize the removal of children from their LGBT parents.

PROJECT MISSION:

1) Notre but est de développer la conscience du grand public sur la situation en Russie et de créer une perspective positive de l'histoire LGBT russe.

2) Pour les russes: montrer des personnages LGBTQ iconiques de leur histoire pour montrer que l'homosexualité n'est pas une influence de l'Ouest.

3) Pour les autres: Changer la façon dont l'Ouest exprime sa solidarité pour ne pas contrarier les russes, spécialement les LGBT et leurs sympathisants.

4) Se concentrer sur la vie intime de ses personnages dont les russes sont fiers. Leur orientation sexuelle est au coeur des images, comme sources de leurs motivations et pourtant impossible de la nier.

5) Pour créer un meilleur monde il faut l'imaginer avant. On leur donne un coup de main.

6) Participer à arrêter / retarder l'avancement de l'homophobie en Russie, surtout les nouvelles lois visant à limiter les droits humains des personnes LGBT et de leurs enfants.

7) Une partie des profits des ventes de l'oeuvre lors des expositions serait donné à la LGBTQ Network en Russie. lgbtnet.ru/en

REACH-OUT PROGRAM

On compte exposer le projet dans le plus de villes possibles. Ces expositions serviront à créer des centres concentrateurs de gens informés qui pourraient partager le projet. Ces expositions auraient pour but aussi d'établir un dialogue avec des artistes russes en exposant leurs oeuvres ou en faisant des conférences pour le public.

Avec nos partenaires on a réussi à distribuer notre projet à plus de deux millions de personnes de la communauté LGBT, dont 200 000 à Moscou.

Collaborations avec la presse et blogues pertinents (pas uniquement de la communauté LGBT).

PROJECT MISSION:

1) Our goal is to develop awareness in the general public about the situation in Russia and to create a positive and accurate out-view of LGBT Russian History.

2) For Russians, we want to show iconic LGBT figures from their History to demonstrate how homosexuality is not an 'influence' from the West.

3) For the rest of the world, we want to change the way the West expresses its solidarity to avoid antagonizing the Russian public, especially the LGBT community and their supporters.

4) To concentrate on the intimate lives of these characters of whom Russians are proud. The sexual orientation of these characters is at the heart of the images, as a source of their raison d'être, personalities, achievement and struggles. It is impossible to hide or negate this orientation.

5) To create a better world, one needs to imagine it first. We want to give LGBT Russians a hand with that.

6) Participate, even if it's minimally, to stop the advancement of homophobia in Russia and elsewhere.

REACH-OUT PROGRAM

Our idea is to reach as many people as possible trough exhibitions, conferences, social media and of course this book.

With our partners, the application Hornet and the magazine Depesha, we have had a reach of 2 million people trough the world, from those 2 hundred thousand in Moscow.

We hope that this project reaches other artists and inspires them, people outside the LGBT community and informs them, that it opens minds, creates compassion and that it touches many hearts.

CREDITS

Photographer and Art Director: Damian Siqueiros
Communications and production assistant: Diana Gonzalez
Stylist: Sophia Graziani
Make-up artist: Olivier Vinet
Hair stylist: Cathy L
Background painting and masks: Daniel Barkley
First assistant: Bérenger Zyla
Assistant to styling and Make-up: Camille Sabbagh
Assistance team: Liliana Ortiz, Gigiola Caceres, Sebastien Beaupre
Behind the scenes images: Guillermo Castellanos, Mateo H. Casis, Bérenger Zyla
Behind the scenes editing: Guillermo Castellanos
Communication collaborator: Antoine Aubert
Special collaborators: Arnaud Baty, Ari Vilhjalmsson
Agent: Patricia Doss (zetaproduction.com)

Characters / Models:

Pyotr Ilyich Tchaikovsky: Stephen Amnotte
Akeksey Sofornov: Antonio Bavaro
Anna Yevreinova: Evelyne-Louise Bergeron
Maria Feodorova: Claire Crombrez
Sergei Diaghilev: Miguel Doucet
Vaslav Nijinsky: Roscoe Stone
Policewoman: Rachel Salzman
Olympic Athlete: Antonia Dolhaine
Stalin impersonator: Sebastien Beaupre
Putin impersonator: Tristan Harris

DAMIAN SIQUEIROS is an internationally-acclaimed award-winning photographer and visual artist. Born in Northwest Mexico, currently residing in Montreal, Canada and a citizen of the world, Damian's first mission as an artist is being 'human-e' by incorporating a sense of social conscience that betters our life and our social environment into his images, artistic or editorial. One of the goals of his work is to expose the constructed and performative character of identity and their imposition by social and political constructs.

He feels particularly invested in the search for Beauty and the transformative power art has to change our surroundings or our appreciation of it. He wields this power to achieve a positive and harmonious view of the world that he can share with his public.

Winner of the *Public's Choice Scotia Bank Prize* 2010 in Montreal's *Art Souterrain*, Damian has exhibited in museum and galleries in Mexico, Spain, Paris, New York (*The Gabarron Foundation*), Washington D.C. (*Art Museum of the Americas*) and nationwide in Canada; and collaborated with international magazines and clients including *Vogue Mexico, Elle, Esquire, Porrua* and *Les Grands Ballets Canadiens of Montreal*.

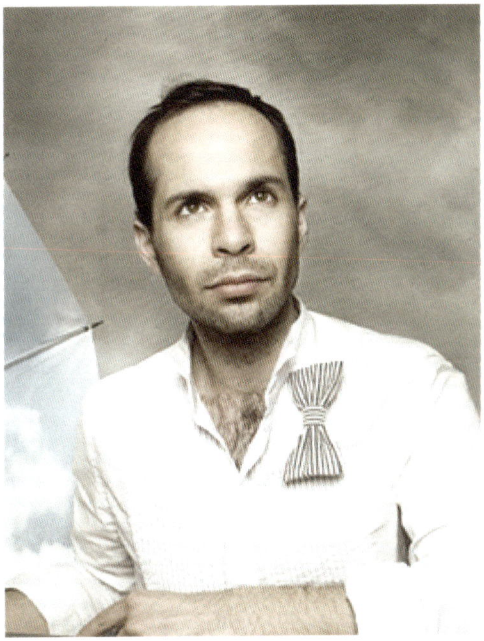

CPSIA information can be obtained at www.ICGtesting.com
Printed in the USA
LVIW01n0749120615
442179LV00007B/18